I AM ENOUGH

90 Days of Spiritual Nuggets to Recognize and Embrace Your Authentic Self

Harold Leffall, Jr.
Zaire Publishing

Notice

Mention of specific authorities in this book does not imply they endorsed this book.

Copyright 2018 by Harold Leffall

All rights reserved. No part of this publication may be reproduced or transmitted in any form or by any means, electronic or mechanical, including photocopying, recording, or any other information storage and retrieval system, without the written permission of the publisher.

Printed in the United States of America.

Library of Congress Cataloging-in-Publication Data
Leffall, Harold

I AM ENOUGH: 90 Days of Spiritual Nuggets to Recognize and Embrace Your Authentic Self

Dedicated to You

May you always remember the truth that you are enough.

Acknowledgements

Johann Wolfgang von Goethe once said, "Whatever you think you can do or believe you can do, begin it. Action has magic, grace and power in it." None of us achieves any measure of success or fulfillment without the love, support and encouragement of others. A special thanks to those who have shown up for me when I forgot I was enough – Wanda L Floyd, Zaire Christopher Leffall, Beverley Wilson, Anthony Scott Davis, Tamara Jacques, Gwendolyn Lucas, Thurston Jackson, Larry Turner, Paula Robinson, Babette Karsseboom, Johnny and Betty Robinson, Barbara "Jean" Tappan, Hazel "Renee" Dixon, Tommy Lee Hooks, Fred Busby, Mishal Boscana, Lauren Robinson, Colette Hill, Ron Steele, Jackie Drake, Chauncey Winn, Verlenda Sutton, and Harold Leffall, Sr. Thank you to the readers and audiences who have encouraged me to continue encouraging them.

FOREWORD

Have you ever wondered why the people who say they love you are the ones who will leave and reject you? I have. From childhood, I suffered from low self-esteem and rejection. I was adopted at the age of 11 months. I loved my parents, but they hurt me. At age 16, I lost my mother due to a massive heart attack. Her loss left me feeling abandoned once again by a mother. Merely a month after her death, my father began dating another woman. I was often left alone a lot to raise myself. The first Thanksgiving holiday after my mom died, my dad purchased a dinner for me from the grocery store. He spent the day with his girlfriend while I spent the day sitting alone, crying and wondering why I wasn't good enough or important enough for my dad to stay home and spend the day with me.

Most days I felt unwanted, abandoned, and scared. I was shy, and used shyness as a way to escape from socializing with others. Actually, I was more afraid of not fitting in, of people not liking me, or hurting me and abandoning me all over again. From childhood to adulthood, the reoccurring thoughts of not being good enough haunted me. I was very insecure, but I hid it well. I loved to sing, teach, and speak in front of others. In order to do that, I had to teach myself to appear confident. If only people knew the truth behind my false confidence. Every time I was presented with the opportunity, I gladly agreed to perform while

in my mind I wrestled with an array of thoughts: Can I really do this? What if I forget everything I know? What if they don't like me? What if they find out how scared I really am? My life was a façade, just like that of so many others.
We fight daily to fit in or measure up to what we perceive as success. We are in a constant search for happiness thinking it will come in the form of the perfect spouse, the kind of car we drive, the clothes we wear, and our social status. Why? Because society tells us that ordinary isn't good enough. The normal person goes to college, earns a degree, starts his career, purchases a house, gets married, has 2.5 children and a dog. This is the society's definition of being happy and successful.

But what about your dreams? No time for that. Dreaming is for risk takers and fools. Dreams do not feed your family. How many of us have given up on our dreams or talked ourselves out of going after our dreams and visions because we are afraid we do not have what it takes, it costs too much money, no one will come or buy it. One thinks to himself, Why would anyone listen to me? They will listen, buy it, and come because you have what it is needed. The world is waiting on you - your idea, your book, your bakery, your invention. Your purpose and destiny are waiting for you to realize how important YOU ARE! No one can do what you're supposed to do. Regardless of how many people already have or are already doing it, YOU have a contribution to make. Your past does not determine your future. Whether you were adopted, sexually abused, or abandoned.

Whether you grew up in foster care, your mother was on drugs, or your father walked out on you. Yes, he abused you. Yes, the marriage failed and now you're divorced. You still can have everything you ever dreamed of. It's yours and tangible the moment you realize that "I am enough!" Everything you need to be successful was placed inside you at birth. You just have to believe in yourself. The day I silenced my past was the day I began to live on purpose.

Today, my mission is to help others realize their potential and live life to the fullest. Love who you are. Love every hurt, painful experience, and disappointment. Those situations serve to teach, strengthen, and shape us. Now allow them to show you that you have what it takes to make your vision a reality. You are enough, and the world is waiting on you. Give yourself permission to be great!!! I believe in you.

~ Wanda L. Floyd

Dear Authentic Self,

I have lived most of my life trying to fit in, to make others comfortable, and yearning for acceptance. Although, at times, it felt like my attempts were yielding the desired results, I lost my sense of self. I lost the self who dreamed bigger than my circumstances. I lost the self that was confident, eager, and alive. I became a person who learned to live in a state of discontent. I learned to forego my dreams and ambitions to fit the image others held of me. I put others' needs above my own. I settled into the reality that I would always come up short. Short on purpose, money, relationships, and love. I learned to settle and become comfortable with the discontent that was my constant reality. To some, it may have appeared that I was doing well as I often wore my mask with a smile. The smile was a deflection to distract others from seeing all the pain that I allowed to rest in my soul because I did not know I could live in freedom and remove the mask. To do the latter would have meant that I'd lose the false identity those closest to me had grown accustomed to.
But today, I choose me. I choose to live in the truth that I am worthy. I choose to live in the truth that my dreams do matter. I choose to live in the truth that I no longer have to settle for that which does not serve my highest good. I welcome me back to myself.

I AM ENOUGH.
'I am enough' answers everything. Every doubt, every fear, and every insecurity is resolved with that powerful declaration.

Day 1

"You are on a journey of transformation. You are exploring the wisdom of your soul. You are shedding old beliefs and stories that no longer fit who you are becoming. Be brave, dear one. You are stepping onto your authentic path."
~Laurel Bleadon-Maffei

Letting Go...

The reality is that I can change my life in an instant. At the very moment I make a decision to break free from my old storyline, I set the atmosphere for a new beginning—one that is not hindered or diminished by my past. I can let go of all the wrongdoings I have initiated, as well as those executed by others. I step out of the past and live in the present with no residue of what I have been through, no remnant of influence from those who hurt me or the mistakes I have made. I am able to move forward as a stronger individual due to a fresh start that is fueled by new information and greater revelation. I understand that I'm not merely the sum of my actions. Only I can first define the weight or significance things have in my life. To know that I'm not who people say or think I am is liberating—no need to entertain or seek affirmation from others who seek to dictate how I feel. I am the thermostat in my life. A thermostat regulates. While others may condemn, judge, or attack, I do not have to be affected by this. I set the temperature of what matters in my life.

I set the tone of my life.
I AM ENOUGH.

Day 2

"When you fight to cling to people who are no longer meant to be in your life, you delay your destiny. Let them go."
~Mandy Hale

Transformation.

When I aim to change my life to reflect my truth, I may hope for an immediate, radical change. However, transformation is a process. It is about embracing a new way of being and living. Real transformation often happens without much noticeable external change in the beginning. Before the caterpillar becomes the butterfly, it develops a chrysalis. This is the process of being prepared and nurtured to emerge as a new and beautiful creation. On the surface, it may not look like much is happening, but the delicate chrysalis process transforms the fuzzy caterpillar into a vibrant, beautiful butterfly with wings of intricate design and intense colors. If I am willing, I too can experience a "chrysalis" type of transformation in which the old self becomes no longer recognizable as my true self emerges.

I trust the process.
I AM ENOUGH.

Day 3

"There comes a day when you realize turning the page is the best feeling in the world, because you realize there is so much more to the book than the page you were stuck on."
~Zyan Malik

The Power Within...

As I free myself from the beliefs, expectations, and values of others, I can live in my fullness. My misery and pain are often related to my futile attempts to live a lie and be who I am not, which causes me pain. Being inauthentic separates me from the power that lies within, as true power does not come from outside of me. I have suffered because I believed that my power was tied to my job, bank accounts, education, and relationships. In reality, my power is my awareness of my connection to the Creator. As I live in this awareness, I tap into a self-sustaining strength that is not dictated by external circumstances. I live life with poise and confidence because I understand that what lives within me can never be altered or changed, including when my external life is interrupted and distorted by human experiences. Therefore, I will not lose my power if my job ends. I will not lose my power if my finances decline. I will not lose my power when a relationship ends. I only appear to lose power when I attempt to hold onto what was. When I look to outside sources to give me fulfillment, I give my power away.

I have the power.
I AM ENOUGH.

Day 4

"One day, you will wake up and there won't be any more time to do the things you've always wanted. Do it now."
~Paulo Coelho

Embracing Change…

Anatole France says, "All changes, even the most longed for, have their melancholy; for what we leave behind is part of ourselves; we must die to one life before we can enter into another." Everyone suffers in varying degrees from cainotophobia, which is simply the fear of change or newness. The truth is, I stagnate my life by holding firmly to what was. I stay bound to yesterday when I resist the new realities that life offers and settle in situations that no longer serve a purpose for my destiny. As a result, life often has pushed me forward with those unwelcome disturbances before change occurs. Rather than initiate the change my heart's desire was leading me toward, I typically sat idly until situations beyond my control shook me from my familiar place. In the meantime, I remained in unfulfilling spaces longer than I should and stayed in toxic relationships longer than I need to. In my resistance, I traded my destiny for complacency by settling for situations that were only meant to be temporary. But today, I am ready for a change.

I will no longer settle for less.
I AM ENOUGH.

Day 5

"It's not what you look at that matters, it is what you see."
~Henry David Thoreau

Until Today...

I have allowed guilt and shame to run my life. Somewhere deep in the recesses of my consciousness, I was always looking for things to fall apart. This was steeped in my erroneous belief that I was unworthy. This is why, when things were going well, I had the tendency to brace myself for adversity. I held the flawed conviction that I would be punished for the so-called wrongs I had committed. I never really permitted myself to simply live in the space of abundance and peace, which are my birthright. The moment some unwanted occurrence would happen in my life, I viewed it as evidence of the punishment I deserved. Thus, the battle in my mind began. This explains why I would have periods of plenty followed by ones of deprivation. Until today, I never realized how the root of the lack I experienced was caused by my consciousness of feeling unworthy. I never considered how my thoughts cultivated the landscape of my reality. At my core, I never believed I was enough. I know now that I am a beloved expression of God. I no longer need to be afraid when fearful thoughts arise—I acknowledge them as false programming and move on. I know now that my responsibility is to keep my predominant thoughts on the things I desire. As I allow my mind to steer clear of judgment and negativity, I remember that I am worthy just as I am.

I am worthy.
I AM ENOUGH.

Day 6

"Logic will get you from A to B. Imagination will take you everywhere."
~Albert Einstein

Dream Again...

I sense myself expanding and growing in love. I see the manifestation of my dreams and aspirations. I know that I am creating my experiences with my thoughts. I feel blessings all around. I know that, as I focus on blessings, more will flow through and to me. I am so happy with this awareness, and thankful that I can see the light in all things. I am divinely guided and supremely protected in love. I love this life just as it is. I am expecting things to get better continuously. I focus on the light, and as I do, darkness becomes a mere shadow. Thank you, God, and so it is.

I shall welcome my blessings.
I AM ENOUGH.

Day 7

"Never be afraid to trust an unknown future to a known God."
~Corrie ten Boom

I Believe...

Faith is believing that life is on our side including when what is happening to us is not making sense. Believing is a verb, and a verb denotes action. To say that I believe and then not act is synonymous with mental assent. Believing is receiving in Spirit before it is manifested in the physical. Nothing is accomplished without belief. Hope anticipates something that cannot be had until God brings it to pass. The law of life is belief. As I think, that is what I experience. The light of faith allows me to move through this life experience unencumbered. When I quiet my mind, I tap into a power that is not limited by my five senses. This internal power allows me to see the invisible. Faith is evidenced in every human being. For some, the light of faith is dim; however, I need but turn it up to experience the very substance for which I hope. Faith releases what was already present. It allows God's energy to move in my life. Faith is getting up in spite of how down I feel. It is moving forward when I would rather remain still. It is trusting in God that all things are truly working out for my benefit when I do not yet see the physical evidence.

I believe and let go.
I AM ENOUGH.

Day 8

"There are two mistakes one can make along the road to truth... not going all the way, and not starting."
~Buddha

I Decide...

Today, I choose to live better, to be more courageous, more loving, and more abundant. I may, for years, have lived out the fears of the past. I now know that I am not a victim of any circumstance that may have previously kept me derailed from going forward. Whatever I encountered, I now recognize that I have the ability to redefine my experiences in a different way that is life-affirming. I understand that growth can sometimes be difficult, but the benefits always outweigh the pain. Armed with new information, knowledge, and understanding, I no longer follow the same patterns that made my life chaotic and draining in the past.

Congratulations to me on my new beginning!
I AM ENOUGH.

Day 9

"A man is but the product of his thoughts. What he thinks, he becomes."
~Mahatma Ghandi

Renewing My Mind...

I see what I have been conditioned to see. Renewing my mind allows me to release old, worn-out beliefs that have kept me bound to the past. It has been said that the images we hold steadfast in our minds over the years are not illusions; they are patterns by which we are able to mold our destiny. For too long, many people have replayed the same negative tapes over and over in their minds that say they are not good enough, not worthy of their heart's desires, or even worse, encouraging them to hold the belief that something was inherently wrong with them. These false thoughts, often planted in my mind by unhealthy individuals, have caused me to feel dehydrated by life. Ultimately, what I am seeking through transformation is my true self. At the core of every human being is the need to discover who they really are. My goal is to come back to myself and to live my truth as I know it, rather than to live in a way that makes others comfortable. I recently heard a caller on a talk radio program who called in to offer these wise words: "I'd rather be hated for who I am rather than be loved for who I am not."

I am who I am.
I AM ENOUGH.

Day 10

"You have to go the way your blood beats. If you don't live the only life you have, you won't live some other life, you won't live any life at all."
~James Baldwin

Begin Again…

The beauty of life is that no matter where I am, I can always begin anew. I may have experienced a period of horrific loss and change, but my heartbeat reveals to me that I can start anew from my current position. Each day I am reborn—armed with fresh insight and strengthened by life's adversity—I am encouraged by my survival, which informs me that I am more than a conqueror.

Today, I choose to stand in my power.
I AM ENOUGH.

Day 11

"What is not started today is never finished tomorrow."
~Johann Wolfgang von Goethe

Divine Boldness...

I'm willing to be radical and bold with the vision I have been given. Goethe said of boldness that it has "genius, power and magic in it." Life takes on new meaning when I live with the internal assurance that, whatever the case may be, I am divinely guided and protected. With this awareness, I can live the more abundant life Jesus spoke into me. I no longer shrink from life when it presents new challenges, but I press boldly forward toward my vision in spite of the dismal appearance of things. I rest in the assurance that divine protection is my birthright and I can press on, confidently knowing that I have the power to make it.

I know and believe.
I AM ENOUGH.

Day 12

"Don't look further for answers: be the solution. You were born with everything you need to know. Make a promise to stop getting in the way of the blessing that you are. Take a deep breath, remember to have fun, and begin."
~Jonathan H. Ellerby

Time to Heal...

I must stop recreating my pain in new relationships. Too often, I bring my old self-defeating patterns into new relationships and I am left wondering why my life is unfulfilled. The answer is that I continue to hold on to past hurts that I have never allowed to heal. I heal my pain through acknowledgment and forgiveness: I acknowledge the times in my life when I was wounded, which created in me fear, panic, and attachment. I acknowledge the individuals who may have mistreated or abused me because of their own need for healing. Breathe deeply, because for many of us, the pain has been so deep for so long, the thought of it all is overwhelming. I will follow my breath, remind myself that I am ready to grow and let this pain go. Then, I shall simply forgive myself first for acting in ways that were not always in my best interests. I'll forgive myself for the pain I inflicted on myself and others. I'll forgive those who have caused me pain, irrespective of how great or small. The act of forgiveness allows me to be set free

I am deserving...I am powerful.
I AM ENOUGH.

Day 13

"You don't need endless time and perfect conditions. Do it now. Do it today. Do it for twenty minutes and watch your heart start beating."
~Barbara Sher

Power...

The journey I have embarked on is about living a life of authenticity and power. What is Power? Power is the force of creation and transformation within that allows me to manifest my reality. It is my ability to create the life I was meant to live—a life of purpose, joy, and absolute fulfillment. I was born to win, to conquer, and to rise above challenges, not to be overcome by them.

I stand in my power.
I AM ENOUGH.

Day 14

"Begin today. Declare out loud to the universe that you are willing to let go of struggle and eager to learn through joy."
~Sarah Ban Breathnach

Renewed Spirit...

Life is a constant cycle of new beginnings. As I go through periods when I feel as though I have lost my way, every new day, every moment offers me the opportunity to re-create. I create new life when I experience a shift in my perception—including the ways in which I experience adversity will no longer be a struggle. It is never about how intense the adversity is; my power lies in how I perceive it. When I rightly perceive a situation, I am at ease, even in the midst of what looks like a storm to others.

I am strengthened in adversity.
I AM ENOUGH.

Day 15

"As long as man stands in his own way, everything seems to be in his way."
~Ralph Waldo Emerson

Embracing Change...

Everything must change; nothing stays the same. Life is ever changing. There are times in my life when change is not an option—it is a reality. During times when my life is punctuated by normal changes and I fall into fear and disbelief, I have a choice to either embrace the shift or resist it. When I resist change, I create suffering. On the other hand, when I embrace those natural occurrences that happen in everyone's life—the pain of losing a loved one, the shock of being terminated from a job, the emptiness from ending a relationship—I open the way for new mercies and blessings.

Life is on my side.
I AM ENOUGH.

Day 16

"Throughout human history, our greatest leaders and thinkers have used the power of words to transform our emotions, to enlist us in their causes, and to shape the course of destiny. Words cannot only create emotions, they create actions. And from our actions flow the results of our lives."
~Tony Robbins

Speak Life...

I create impressions in my subconscious mind through verbal expression. My words are powerful tools. I shape my life experiences through my power center—my voice. Words are infused with both power and energy. They reflect what I believe and are charged with spiritual force. Words carry vibrations that affect the mood of my environment. I can create a heaven or hell right here on earth through my words. Scripture tells me, "In the beginning was the Word, and the Word was with God, and the Word was God. And the Word was made flesh." The changes I seek are in the words I speak. The scripture instructs me to, "Call those things that be not as though they were." When I arrive at a place in my life when I desire something different, I must speak life into it. Throughout scripture, prior to God creating anything, He spoke it, and it was so.

So today, I will use my power and speak only of the good things I desire.
I AM ENOUGH.

Day 17

"Anything man can imagine, man can make real."
~Jules Verne

A New Chapter...

I know that I have created my reality with the thoughts I hold in my head and heart. I am not a victim of circumstance. I am not what I have been through. I use every challenge, set-back, and break down as the trigger to become stronger. I am not ashamed of what I have been through; it has all worked to awaken my purpose. I shape my reality with how I perceive things. I see an opportunity for growth in everything, including experiences that I would have previously called negative or painful. My mind is an energy field with the capacity to create the things I truly desire.

I elevate my thoughts.
I AM ENOUGH.

Day 18

"Do what you can, with what you have, where you are."
~Theodore Roosevelt

The Rhythm of Life...

What is absolutely true is that life is a fulfilling journey. My life is like a dance where at times I get off beat or out of sync as I find my way back to the rhythm. As I learn to surrender to the music of my life, I learn the art of flowing with the beat of the Universe. I do not know exactly what tomorrow will bring, but I do know that all things work together for my own good. No matter how bleak things may appear at times, I can rest assured that this, too, shall pass. I realize that as I live from my heart (power center), I understand that there is a power and a presence that can lead me out of pain to power. There are no accidents. Life does not just happen. There is a purpose and reason for all I experience. I am guided, whether I know it or not, whether willingly or not, toward growth. During moments when I briefly forget who I am in the now and begin to repeat old patterns and behaviors, I should simply remind myself gently, "I do not behave as such anymore; I no longer react in fear when things do not turn out the way I expect; I no longer panic when an unexpected bill comes and it exceeds what may be in my bank account; I no longer seek the approval of others or act in ways that do not honor who I am.

I move to my own beat.
I AM ENOUGH.

Day 19

"When you commit yourself to living love, you feel at peace with yourself because you are at harmony with the flow of life. Viewing life from the highest perspective, you feel confident and secure. You realize that regardless of how things appear, you are loved and protected. Knowing you are one with God, you have peace with you wherever you go. You're not looking for love, but for opportunities to love."
~Susan L. Taylor

Self-Care...

Every morning, I awaken to the reality that I have a choice. I can choose to love myself first before I give any part of myself away. Or I can decide to step out into the world empty and allow situations, circumstances, and people to dictate how I feel. I choose to spend the beginning of my day in gratitude and appreciation of myself, seeking opportunities to love on and encourage myself. As I love myself with words of appreciation and affirmation, my cup is filled. I say what I mean and mean what I say. I appreciate the positive affirmation or compliments others give me but that does not change my day. Loving me, I realize, is my responsibility. As I love myself fully, I show others how to love me.

I love me.
I AM ENOUGH.

Day 20

"As a man thinketh in his heart so is he."
~James Allen

Thoughts Become Things...

Everything starts in the mind. The mind is my center of creativity, from the new technologies I enjoy to the conditions I choose to live in. My thoughts, then, create my reality. Whatever I focus my mind on I attract into being. If my thoughts are primarily on lack and limitation, I will draw those experiences into reality. Conversely, having my mindset on abundance, I will manifest more of increase. The mind is a powerful tool. My thoughts are like living magnets – drawn to me from that which is in me. Jesus said, "As thou hast believed so be it done unto thee." The truth is thoughts become things.

I change my thoughts...I change my life.
I AM ENOUGH.

Day 21

"When I let go of what I am, I become what I might be."
~Lao Tzu

I Surrender...

In life, there is either resistance or surrender. Resistance leads to suffering, while surrender ushers in peace. Resistance is the decision to act alone; surrender is the decision to act with God. When I surrender, I am content with what is. I cease from seeking joy from external things—I simply allow the joy that is already within me to be released. I have the capacity to redirect the story of my life. Unbounded from my past experiences, I can change the blueprint of my life by changing my mind. When I change my perception, and understand that everything in my life happens for a divine reason, I respond rather than react to life. To respond places the power within me. There is security in knowing that the Universe is always on my side. The key is to remember.

I am whole and complete.
I AM ENOUGH.

Day 22

"All I have seen teaches me to trust the Creator for all I have not seen."
~Ralph Waldo Emerson

I Choose Faith...

The way I arrest fear is through refocusing my thoughts to those things I desire. I know that whatever I focus on grows. If I focus on not fearing something, my focus remains on that which I do not want and I keep the experience alive. Not living in fear requires daily attention. It requires spending regular time simply being still, so I can connect to the wisdom within me. I can redirect my thoughts by writing down my hopes, reading inspirational material, listening to uplifting music, and using positive affirmations. As I shift my focus, I loosen the grip of fear. Refocusing my thoughts to a higher (positive) vibration shifts my mood. As my mood is shifted, my faith is activated. By keeping myself engaged in positive activities, I eliminate the entryway for fear. Napoleon Hill says that, "Positive and negative emotions cannot occupy the mind at the same time. One or the other must dominate. It is your responsibility to make sure that positive emotions constitute the dominating influence in your mind."

I will work my faith.
I AM ENOUGH.

Day 23

"With God, you are stronger than your struggles and more fierce than your fears. God provides comfort and strength to those who trust in Him. Be encouraged, keep standing, and know that everything's going to be alright."
~Germany Kent

Activated...

Being able to let go is faith in action. Anytime I cannot let something go—be it a relationship, job, or anger—I am living in fear. Living in faith empowers me because I know that what is for me cannot be taken away. If a person leaves, let him or her go. Letting go is an act of faith, and an act of power in which I free myself from attachment. I lose personal power when I feel that, if something changes, I will be hindered or broken. I lose my way by trying to hold on to things that are not meant for my highest good. This is often a difficult pill to swallow as I believe I know what is best for my life. The reality is, God is always leading me forward, and sometimes I do not want to move.

I will keep the faith. I will take action.
I AM ENOUGH.

Day 24

"What lies behind you and what lies in front of you, pales in comparison to what lies inside of you."
~Ralph Waldo Emerson

My Lesson...

Somewhere along my journey, I lost my way. I forgot everything I thought I knew about faith, peace, and love. I stopped dreaming and found myself simply going through the motions of life, devoid of hope and joy. What I now know is that when I allowed relationships, people, and situations to dictate my reality, I had simply forgotten who I was. It took every challenge and obstacle I encountered for me to realize that real transformation comes from within and that I had the power to recreate my reality. Now I realize that I do not have to live with fear, that I can choose faith, and that my words are powerful. Were it not for those difficult moments, I would not know the release of simply embracing change rather than holding onto what was. I would not know the significant impact divine connection has on how I saw myself and the world around me. Were it not for the periods of lack and limitation in my life, I would never have become aware that living abundantly is not only about how much money I have, but about finding the courage to live authentically. Through it all, I am now aware that each day I am given a new beginning to live better.

I love who I am becoming.
I AM ENOUGH.

Day 25

"Document the moments you feel most in love with yourself - what you're wearing, who you're around, what you're doing. Recreate and repeat."
~Warsan Shire

I Am Loved...

When life feels void of meaning; When the darkness appears greater than the light; When life appears to be crumbling around you; When your mind is convoluted with fear and despair; When family and friends are nowhere to be found... There is a place where fulfillment rests. A place where joy abounds. That place of light and love is within.

I was born from love.
I AM ENOUGH.

Day 26

"You have been criticizing yourself for years, and it hasn't worked. Try approving of yourself and see what happens."
~Louise L. Hay

God Reigns...

The Greek playwright Aeschylus said, "He who learns must suffer." Pain is information. It offers me life lessons and makes my life deeper and more meaningful. A scripture that I often refer to during challenging times reads, "After you have suffered a while, God will restore." I am reminded here that whatever I am going through will not last always, and that God will use my trials to strengthen me for greater things.

I will embrace the lesson and wake up to my power.
I AM ENOUGH.

Day 27

"Until you value yourself, you won't value your time. Until you value your time, you will not do anything with it."
~M. Scott Peck

Self-Love...

When I love myself, all of my relationships are enhanced. There is a tendency of wanting to assume the role of making others feel better while neglecting my own self-care. It is not my responsibility to attempt to make others happy. My commitment must always be to make sure I am honoring myself and giving myself the love I mistakenly looked to others to give me. Poet Mari Evans says, "I will bring you a whole person and you will bring me a whole person and we will have twice as much love and everything."

I live in my truth.
I AM ENOUGH.

Day 28

"What lies behind us and what lies before us are tiny matters compared to what lies within us."
~Ralph Waldo Emerson

Divine Connections...

Every living soul comes from God, who made me both human and divine. There is an interdependence that connects us. It is through my connections to others that I gain a clearer perspective of who I am. As unique as I am, I am not able to master this life journey alone. I need other people. I need the engagement of others to illuminate the truth of who I am. Most have heard the adage, "When the student is ready, the teacher will appear." It has also been said, "No man is your enemy, no man is your friend, every man is your teacher." Everyone I invite into my life will teach me something—these interactions are divine connections. Sometimes the learning is easily welcomed, such as a gentle word of encouragement from a stranger during a time of confusion. Other times the lesson may come from a harsh supervisor who pushes me to leave a job I never liked. These divinely orchestrated connections move me beyond my self-imposed limitations. Whether it is to teach me how to love, how to be more courageous, or how to step out in faith, every relationship has the potential to make me a better person.

Life is on my side.
I AM ENOUGH.

Day 29

"Self-care is never a selfish act—it is simply good stewardship of the only gift I have, the gift I was put on earth to offer to others."
~Parker Palmer

The Process...

Why do I avoid change? I do so because it is unfamiliar, and I associate this with being in the dark, as well as destruction. In actuality, however, birthing occurs in the dark. Truthfully, life is a process of going through the dark to arrive into the light. It is in the darkness that development occurs. When I go through dark moments, I'm being pushed toward faith. Living faith is active, it is an evolving awareness of truth. Webster defines process as a natural phenomenon marked by gradual change that leads toward a particular result. Often, in life, before a major breakthrough, I experience profound loss or challenges. In fact, at the nexus of going to my next level in life, circumstances often appear as though I am digressing. Yet, I can persevere, learn the lesson, and blessings always follow.

I will remain steadfast, for my breakthrough is near.
I AM ENOUGH.

Day 30

"No one can make you feel inferior without your consent."
~Eleanor Roosevelt

Be Still...

How do I get through the dark days of my life? I simply surrender to stillness. There is a calmness within that knows no pain, fear or suffering. I access this place, my divine self, when I become "still." It is my divine self that gives me peace through the storm. Surrendering to stillness allows me to know that, in spite of appearances, all is well. I acknowledge that I cannot control anything but my thoughts and actions.

Be still and know.
I AM ENOUGH.

Day 31

"Because one believes in oneself, one doesn't try to convince others. Because one is content with oneself, one doesn't need others' approval. Because one accepts oneself, the whole world accepts him or her."
~Lao-Tzu

Truth is...

So much of how I live my life journey has been rooted in what I am told and have observed in my youth. Those early experiences created thinking patterns about living that shaped my reality. I have become who I am based on how I was treated and what I was told, during those formative years, from my parents and those who had access to me. Early experiences taught me who I thought I was supposed to be. Often, I lived out these manufactured roles for years, being a person I was not, while my heart called me to awaken to the truth of my being. I found myself living life on a tireless treadmill of activity, always running after but not arriving at a place of fulfillment. Until, finally, I came to myself with the truth that the way I've been living did not work for me anymore and I developed a thirst to discover who I really am. The truth is, I am a divine original created by God on purpose, for a purpose.

My life matters.
I AM ENOUGH.

Day 32

"People are like stained-glass windows. They sparkle and shine when the sun is out, but when the darkness sets in their true beauty is revealed only if there is light from within."
~Elisabeth Kübler-Ross

Practicing Forgiveness...

As I connect to myself and allow the healing process to transform me back to love, I discover that the power I had been searching for outside of myself was always within. When I tap into myself, I find wisdom, guidance, and courage. Here, I also discover the peace that surpasses all understanding. To exercise forgiveness toward both myself and others is the only way to clear out toxicity from my body. Toxic emotions are heavy and drain me, preventing me from moving forward. There is no value in holding onto past pain and hurt. Once I no longer hold others accountable for my life, I regain strength. Now, when others bring harm to me through words and deeds, I understand that by forgiving them, I release myself to experience more joy. When I have acted in ways that were not honorable, I now understand that when I forgive myself, I can start anew. Jesus never harbored resentment and animosity toward anyone, including those who crucified Him. He forgave them, which allowed him to walk this earth in full power. I, too, have power when I practice radical forgiveness.

I release and let go.
I AM ENOUGH.

Day 33

"When I loved myself enough, I began leaving whatever wasn't healthy. This meant people, jobs, my own beliefs and habits – anything that kept me small. My judgement called it disloyal. Now I see it as self-loving."
~Kim McMillen

Hope...

In my darkest hours, when I feel like I cannot go on and I feel as though I am going to break, when everything seems against me, in those moments when it feels like I have no options, when my downfall seems imminent, Hope whispers to me, don't give up. You are enough.

I surrender all.
I AM ENOUGH.

Day 34

"Courage is the first of human qualities because it is the quality which guarantees the others."
~Aristotle

No Struggle...

My most profound service to humanity is a return to the innocent truth of my higher calling. It is when I remember who I am that I gain what I thirst for: authenticity. There is no struggle or fear in authenticity. I don't have to wait for others to authorize me to be who I am. I am affirmed with my purpose at birth. When I live out my truth, I am made free. In this freedom, I can live out my God-given authority to experience an abundant life. I realize that I am more than what I see, and I am endowed with the ability to create and recreate that which I desire. God created me. In this knowing, I break the bond of old, self-imposed limitations. I know that whatever I desire I can manifest, first in my mind, then in physical form. I am heir to the kingdom, and no good thing can be withheld from me when I remember this truth.

I am approved by God.
I AM ENOUGH.

Day 35

"She lacks confidence, she craves admiration insatiably. She lives on the reflections of herself in the eyes of others. She does not dare to be herself."
~Anais Nin

God Is...

I have to remind myself when I get that call, or the dreaded notice in the mail, or the doctor's negative report ... that all will be well. It is here when I come to terms with what I choose to believe. Will I allow situations, circumstances, or life's tsunamis to make me forget that God reigns? Or, will I look fear and devastation in the face and declare ... but God!

I will activate my faith today.
I AM ENOUGH.

Day 36

"It is never too late to be what you might have been."
~George Eliot

Living on Purpose...

I am a gift to the Universe – only I can experience my unique genius in this life. To fully know and accept myself right where I am is freeing. Every day, I decide whether to get up or not; to succumb to fear or not, and; to show up authentically or not. Whether or not I embrace this truth, I always have a choice. I remember that I am divinely formed in the same likeness as God, while He allows me to move through life fearlessly. The dilemma for the majority is that we have not been told this before now. I grew up wishing I was different somehow, while never realizing that I was God's unique gift to the world. Each living soul is a divine expression of God's love in action. As I wake up to the divine power that dwells within, I am reborn to my truth.

The choice is mine.
I AM ENOUGH.

Day 37

"The best day of your life is the one on which you decide your life is your own. No apologies or excuses. No one to lean on, rely on, or blame. The gift is yours – it is an amazing journey – and you alone are responsible for the quality of it. This is the day your life really begins."
~Bob Moawad

Rockin my Crown...

It is never too late. The moment I am ready, I can live a new life. As I align my thoughts with my heart, I set in motion a new beginning. I start over and remember the truth of my divinity that I am a piece of God. Now, more than ever, when nothing in the world appears to be stable, I am being called to return to myself for peace and comfort. I know now that everything I see can change in an instant. What can never change is my truth—the essence of who I am and my divine connection to God. I am an heir; I will embrace my royalty. James Baldwin said it best: "Your crown has been bought and paid for. All you have to do is put it on."

I will rock my crown!
I AM ENOUGH.

Day 38

"Courage doesn't happen when you have all the answers. It happens when you are ready to face the questions you have been avoiding your whole life."
~Shannon L. Alder

Ready to Grow…

I must stop recreating pain in new relationships. Too often I bring my old self-defeating patterns into new relationships and wonder why my life is unfulfilled. The answer is that I continue to hold onto past hurts that I have never allowed to heal. I heal my pain through acknowledgment and forgiveness: I acknowledge those times in my life when I was wounded, causing me to go into fear, panic, and attachment. I acknowledge those individuals who may have mistreated or abused me because of their own need for healing. One must breathe deeply, because for many of us the pain has been so deep for so long that the thought alone is overwhelming. I will follow my breath—remind myself that I am ready to grow and let this pain go. And then I simply forgive myself first, for acting in ways that were not always for my highest good. I forgive myself for the pain I inflicted on others. Finally, I forgive those who have caused me pain, no matter how great or small. This act of forgiveness allows me to be healed and set free.

I shall forgive and set myself free.
I AM ENOUGH.

Day 39

"God, when I lose hope, help me to remember that your love is greater than my disappointments, and your plans for my life are better than my dreams."
~Unknown Author

A Divine Original...

I am a divine original, created to make manifest the gifts and talents that the Creator breathed into me to bless the earth. At the core of every human being is the need to rediscover who we really are. To come back to my true self, no longer holding others accountable for my life. Any attempt to make others responsible for my feelings makes me a victim. Accepting the role of victim is my false self; it is not who I am. Even when others have intentionally caused me harm, I have a choice to pick myself up and move forward. Others may have had ill intent toward me, but I am responsible for the way I respond to life. The word 'responsible' comes from a combination of two words: "response" and "able." I may not be able to control outside situations and people, but I can certainly determine my response.

I can control my actions and reactions.
I AM ENOUGH.

Day 40

"It takes courage to grow up and become who you really are."
~E.E. Cummings

I know I am enough when I...

1) Read books to get inspired
2) Am not distracted by the negative opinions of others
3) Make my health a priority
4) Set goals and visualize my success
5) Get back up stronger and wiser after a setback

I commit to always moving forward.
I AM ENOUGH.

Day 41

"You were born with wings. Why prefer to crawl through life?"
~Rumi

I Am Enough...

Fearing that we are not enough is all too common in our culture. Not feeling I am enough often shows up in my life as procrastination, lack of confidence, negative self-talk, comparison, and worry. When I do not know I am enough, I find myself consistently settling in every area of my life—staying on a job I hate, remaining in relationships where I am disrespected, accepting financial lack as normal, and regularly deferring my dreams. Being enough is not based on my appearance, bank account, education, relationship status, zip code, car, the size of my home, etc. The truth is, as a man thinketh, so is he. I was born enough.

I will be true to myself and soar.
I AM ENOUGH.

Day 42

"The most common way people give up their power is by thinking they don't have any"
~Alice Walker

Unapologetically Me...

As I discover my truth, the opinions and beliefs that others have of me have no power over me and how I live. The reality is that, as I take off the mask of deception and rediscover all that I was meant to be, I can clearly see all the false images I once believed—the same ones that made me play small in the world. I now know that I do not need external things to validate me. My birth in the universe is the only validation I need to know that I am worthy. As I remember who I am and whose I am, I'm empowered to live life unapologetically.

I am already whole.
I AM ENOUGH.

Day 43

"Letting go means to come to the realization that some people are a part of your history, but not a part of your destiny."
~Steve Maraboli

My Dreams...

In actuality, every dream is closer than I think. As I accept and live in the truth that all things are working for my good, I no longer have to fear the changes that I experience. I begin to view every challenge simply as a pathway to growth, and I learn to surrender all simply. In surrendering all, I connect with freedom and welcome peace. When I surrender, I am letting go of my need to control that which is beyond my provision. From the outside, surrender may look like a complete breakdown. It may appear I'm giving up when I am actually allowing life to evolve. The truth is, my life is being recalibrated for greater good when I let go and let God take the wheel.

I am moving closer to my dreams.
I AM ENOUGH.

Day 44

"Worthiness had no prerequisites. It's not an If/When proposition. True worthiness is as is."
~Brene Brown

Joy and Pain...

Whatever emotional feelings I radiate is what I will experience. I get what I give my attention to. This is why it is so important that I continually practice self-love and forgiveness. I must refrain from beating myself up with judgmental thoughts about what I should or could have done differently. Self-badgering holds no value and only makes my journey one of bondage. According to Maya Angelou, "'When you know better, you do better." At every moment, I'm doing the very best I can. There is no value in wallowing in self-pity about the past. Forgiveness is the key. I forgive myself and those who have wronged me for I recognize that life is a spiritual symphony of joy and pain.

I give myself permission to be imperfect.
I AM ENOUGH.

Day 45

"Circumstances do not make the man, they reveal him."
~James Allen

I Affirm...

When a word is spoken, it is recorded in the subconscious of both the host and the receiver. All words are formative; they establish the foundation of my life. They are the building blocks of fulfillment. When used properly, my words become the light that leads me on the correct path. They are not simply sound waves but are a spiritual force, infused with the potential to create. God created everything with a word. In the Book of Genesis, the phrase, "And God said" is frequently repeated before every aspect of creation. God gives me a model of how I can bring things to pass through the power of my words. He spoke the entire universe into being. I am created in the image and likeness of God. My words never return to me void, whether they are life-affirming or destructive; they manifest in my life as actual experiences.

I will speak life over my dreams and visions.
I AM ENOUGH.

Day 46

"Man often becomes what he believes himself to be. If I keep on saying to myself that I cannot do a certain thing, it is possible that I may end by really becoming incapable of doing it. On the contrary, if I shall have the belief that I can do it, I shall surely acquire the capacity to do it, even if I may not have it at the beginning."
~Mahatma Gandhi

How Did I Get Here?

Pain can often provide a wealth of information and learning if I am open to the truth. Painful episodes in my life often force me to make major changes and adjustments that I would not otherwise make. Without the pain, I would resign to very static life, never moving away from that which is familiar or comfortable. Questioning and grappling with how I arrived at this place of limited and restricted living becomes my gateway to an awakening. I learn that the misery and pain I have experienced in my life was not due to something or someone outside of myself, but was first created in my thought. There is a cause and effect to everything in the universe. The grace in understanding the source of my beliefs is that I can always change what I believe.

My pain becomes my power.
I AM ENOUGH.

Day 47

"Only in the darkness can you see the stars."
~Martin Luther King Jr.

Life Happens...

Nobody journeys through life unscathed by the complexities of life. Since Biblical times, human beings have experienced suffering and strife. It is a normal part of living. Challenges are not an indication of who I am or what my value is. Life often unfolds in mysterious ways without rational justification. What is true is that everything I go through presents me with an opportunity to either become better or bitter. There is a lesson in all that I endure. In life, there are no wasted experiences. Life is on the side of expansion and unfoldment. This means there will be times of stretching and change if I am to grow into greater awareness. Difficulties and adversity are life's way of offering me an invitation to grow.

I was built to last.
I AM ENOUGH.

Day 48

"We must be willing to get rid of the life we've planned, so as to have the life that is waiting for us. The old skin has to be shed before the new one can come."
~Joseph Campbell

Approved by God...

As difficult as it is, I choose to let go of what others expect me to be. For too long, I have given up my power in an attempt to gain the acceptance of others, which left me disappointed and ashamed. Disappointed because I believed that in order for me to feel happy, I needed the approval of others. Ashamed because I did not like the persona I was acting out. Deep inside, I always knew that in order to live a fulfilling life, I needed to truly care more about how I felt, rather than how others felt about me. Today I know that my responsibility is that I give myself the love that I have mistakenly sought from others. I do this by being true to what is important to me. By saying no when I mean no, and yes only when I mean yes. I release habits, patterns, and behavior that no longer represent the truth about me.

I give myself permission to be me.
I AM ENOUGH.

Day 49

"Ask and you will receive. Seek and you will find; knock, and it will be opened to you."
~Matthew 7:7

I Am Worthy...

The elders remind me that a closed mouth does not get fed. I have gone without because I did not dare to ask for what I wanted. I thought asking made me less than or even selfish. There were times when I didn't ask for what I really wanted because I did not believe I was worthy. What I know now is that no person is more worthy than another. Those who attract and manifest the desires of their heart are those who are bold enough to ask for what they want. Today I know that I can ask the Creator for anything I truly desire. And if my heart and mind align with my integrity, it shall be granted.

I ask and it is given.
I AM ENOUGH.

Day 50

"Success is not final, failure is not fatal: it is the courage to continue that counts."
~Winston S. Churchill

Courage...

Each challenge is an invitation for me to exercise courage in the face of adversity. Every time I act from a place of courage, I experience more peace. I begin to feel a renewal of strength that reminds me I can press forward at times when I am afraid. Courage is a moment-by-moment choice. It is something I must make a conscious effort to demonstrate to myself. I am sending a message to myself that I matter when I act courageously. When I remember that I am worthy, I can conquer my fears and live a life full of courage.

I choose to be courageous.
I AM ENOUGH.

Day 51

"Hope is being able to see that there is light despite all of the darkness."
~Desmond Tutu

New Possibilities...

It is hope that sustains me when everything around me appears to be falling apart. Hope allows me to know that when it appears things are breaking down, a shift and reordering is taking place to align me toward new possibilities. The breakdown experience knocks me off the treadmill of life that allows me to reconsider where I am going. Nobody would choose to go through difficult experiences, but it is those experiences that stretch me and prepare me for more—more joy, more fulfillment, and more abundance. I am unable to experience more if I only have pint-size capacity. Each step along this life journey of continual unfoldment requires that I stretch myself beyond the familiar. To stretch my mind beyond what I think I know. Stretching is simply a part of the process of discovering my full potential. Along that journey, I will fall and stumble at times, but I rise up stronger, bolder, and wiser.

I am ready.
I AM ENOUGH.

Day 52

"God when I lose hope, help me to remember that your love is greater than my disappointments and your plans for my life are better than my dreams."
~Jasmeen Kaur Wadhera

The Law of Belief...

Jesus said, "As thou hast believed so be it done unto thee." My beliefs that rest in my subconscious mind create the experiences that manifest in my life—this is the law of belief. The spiritual laws of life work, whether I am aware of them or not. The law of electricity does not alter neither if it powers the car versus burns down the house, nor if it electrocutes someone versus warming the home. The law simply returns to us the result of the forces that we set in motion through it. Nothing except belief binds us. The root cause of poverty, for instance, is belief. Most people end up in a state of poverty because they are operating out of ineffective beliefs. My pain becomes power when I work my faith and elevate my beliefs.

I believe God.
I AM ENOUGH.

Day 53

"You have to learn to get up from the table when love is no longer being served."
~Nina Simone

Break Free...

I would never willingly place myself in a state of lack or limitation, but when I have thoughts of fear, doubt, and negativity, I attract those experiences to my life. This is the law of cause and effect. What I think, I manifest—nothing just happens. The laws of the universe are always at work. Whether I know them or not, they are operating in my life. There is a cause and effect to everything in the universe.

I got the power.
I AM ENOUGH.

Day 54

"You are never too old to set another goal or dream a new dream."
~C.S. Lewis

Renewing My Mind...

I see what I have been conditioned to see. It has been said that, "The images we hold steadfast in our minds over the years are not illusions; they are patterns by which we are able to mold our destiny." Renewing my mind allows me to release old, worn out beliefs that have kept me bound to the past. For too long, I have replayed the same negative tapes over and over in my mind that say I am not good enough, not worthy of my heart's desires, or worse, that something is inherently wrong with me. These false thoughts, usually planted in my head by unhealthy individuals, have caused me to feel dehydrated by life. Ultimately, what I am seeking through transformation is my true self. At the core of every human being is the need to discover who they really are.

I am transformed by the renewing of my thoughts.
I AM ENOUGH.

Day 55

"You may not control all the events that happen to you, but you can decide not to be reduced by them."
~Maya Angelou

Essence of Love...

Everyone's normal is different. To be different is not negative. What is normal for one person will be abnormal or odd to another. Acknowledging and accepting our differences is the essence of love. I open myself to peace. I must remember that I am divinely human, a physical manifestation of God's love. I long to be in tune with the heartbeat of God, to know His will and purpose for this beautiful gift of life. I know that, when I simply trust, miraculous and wonderful things flow toward me. There is no struggle or pain when I am in a posture of trust. When I am giving to life what I was sent here to share, I bring harmony to the Universe.

I am loved.
I AM ENOUGH.

Day 56

"Faith is taking the first step even when you don't see the whole staircase."
~Martin Luther King, Jr.

FEAR (False Evidence Appearing Real)...

When I'm afraid of something, I actually make the experience real with my imagination. In fact, the effects are experienced in my body through my negative thoughts. Negativity is a mental poison that only infects the host who imagines and holds onto the thought. My nervous system does not distinguish between my thoughts and reality. The dangerous aspect of fear is that if I allow it to go unchecked, I cause the experience of it to become my reality. There is a scripture that reminds me, "that which I fear is upon me." Fear emanates from negativity. I have had the experience of fearing something so intensely, it eventually occurred in my life. I am a powerful being who can create simply by how I think. Choose today to live in faith over fear.

I shall not fear.
I AM ENOUGH.

Day 57

"Hope is being able to see that there is light despite all of the darkness."
~Desmond Tutu

Going Higher...

Accessing hope when life gets tough is the challenge. Hope is always present, but what becomes challenging is tapping into it when life seems to be falling apart. Hope is the belief that things will get better. It is an inner emotion that I have to unleash on my own. Others may help to stimulate the emotion, but to unleash its real power, hope must come from the inside out. To hope is to shift my perspective and find blessings in everything I go through. When I go through the difficulties of life, I must remember that, as long as I have breath in my body, there is hope.

I will never lose hope.
I AM ENOUGH.

Day 58

"How you love yourself is how you teach others to love you"
~Rupi Kaur

Be Still and Know…

The truth is that, when I cease pretending to be who I am not, I am practicing the highest form of love and acceptance. Masks and a façade separate me from my truth. In authenticity, I am truth personified. When I yield to this, I tap into the point of power where all things are possible. I am united with this awareness in stillness. When I allow myself to regularly quiet my mind, the truth is always revealed. The most powerful act that I can engage in is stillness. This act of nothingness is stronger than any exertion using brute force—rather, relax, release, and allow our Spirit to guide us. There is often so much noise in my life that I cannot hear my Spirit's guidance. It is only when the noise is silenced that I receive the guidance I need. When I follow divine guidance, I tap into the ultimate power where all things are possible.

I find truth in stillness.
I Am Enough!

Day 59

"Faith is the bird that feels the light when the dawn is still dark."
~Rabindranath Tagore

Faith It...

Since I do not have perfect faith, I often find myself vacillating from faith to fear. In those moments when I cannot trace God, fear seems to loom large. However, if I can tap into faith rather than fear, I will overcome whatever I am going through. But how do I do that? Sometimes I have to pray myself back to faith. Sing myself back to faith. Meditate myself back to faith. Keep my focus on my faith and not on my fears. In those difficult moments, when I seem to have run out of options, I have to faith it until I make it. Keep believing regardless of the circumstance. I must remember that my breakthrough is closer than it appears.

I trust God.
I AM ENOUGH.

Day 60

"You are not what others think you are. You are what God knows you are."
~Shannon L. Alder

Prayer…

God, let me remember when I lose hope that you are just a prayer away. When I acknowledge You, You are there. When I halt my inner conflict, You are there. When I get still and quiet, You are there. When I remember You, I am assured that I am enough.

God is the source of my strength.
I AM ENOUGH.

Day 61

"Circumstances do not make a man...they reveal him."
~James Allen

Living Abundantly...

I live in an abundant Universe that is filled with all the resources I need to live richly. There is evidence all around me to remind me of the unlimited resources that exist. My heart's desire is to live in the fullness of that which is fruitful. The appearance of lack in my life is merely an illusion created by fear. I am worthy of abundance, and know that anytime I have a need, God will supply.

I was born to live abundantly.
I AM ENOUGH.

Day 62

"Some men see things as they are, and say, Why? I dream of things that never were, and say, "Why not?"
~George Bernard Shaw

Truth Is...

So much of how I live out my life journey has been rooted in what I was told and observed in my youth. Those early experiences created thinking patterns about living that have shaped my reality. I have become who I am based on how I was treated and what I was told during my formative years from my parents and those who had access to me. It is from those experiences that I learned what I thought I was supposed to be. Often, I live out these manufactured roles for years, being someone I was not while my heart called me to awaken to the truth of my being. I found myself living life on a tireless treadmill of activity, always running after but not arriving at a place of fulfillment. Until, finally, I arrived at the truth that the way I've been living did not work for me anymore and I developed a thirst to discover who I really am.

I am free
I AM ENOUGH.

Day 63

"It's the repetition of affirmations that leads to belief. And once that belief becomes a deep conviction, things begin to happen."
~Muhammad Ali

Manifested Faith...

My faith is only made real when I find myself without answers, resources, or connections. Faith is not exemplified while life is going well. Anyone can have faith during a harvest season. Faith is manifested in the dark hours, in those moments when I don't know what to do next, or I have exhausted my options. I learn the most when my life is tested beyond my capacity to fix things. Faith ushers in possibilities. It allows me to tap into a reservoir of strength and creativity that would otherwise remain dormant. In faith, I reimagine my future. Scripture says that without faith, it is impossible to please God. My faith to see my dreams fulfilled is what pleases God.

I have faith...
I AM ENOUGH.

Day 64

"Forgiveness says you are given another chance to make a new beginning."
~Desmond Tutu.

Create Your Breakthrough...

Ideas and thoughts are the seeds of change. It is from this space that I create new experiences. So, I ask you, what are you thinking about? What thoughts do you hold? When you look at your situation, is there a direct relationship between the quality of your life and the things that keep your mind occupied? Renewing my mind means living consciously. The only thing I have absolute control over is my thoughts. Yet, I have allowed the beliefs of others to overly influence how I think. This has led me to a place of emptiness and confusion. The good news is that, as I commit to doing the inner healing of eliminating from my sphere of existence all of the negative dogma from my past, I can awaken to an expansion of awareness of the false ideals I had been operating under. And with this awakening, it is as if my eyes have opened wider and I can see more, thus to realize what has been and is occurring all around me. Oliver Wendell Holmes once stated it this way: "A mind once stretched by a new idea can never go back to its original dimensions."

Nothing changes until I change.
I AM ENOUGH.

Day 65

"Adversity can either break you or make you. The same hammer that breaks the glass also sharpens the steel."
~Bob Johnson

Boldness...

I have to be bold in order to make my dreams a reality. It will require boldness to move out of my comfort zone and decide that, in spite of life challenges and obstacles, I am going to live my dreams. This is by no means an easy task; often, the moment I decide to press forward, I will be confronted with adversity. Boldness is action, not talk. It is making a decision and following through. Boldness is not making a public declaration about what I will do or accomplish, but it is actually doing the work required to realize my dream. Authentic boldness, not arrogance, will propel me forward, even when no one else supports or believes in me. It is boldness that allows me to look beyond my current situation and continue to work toward my dreams with the confidence that the best is yet to come.

I walk the walk.
I AM ENOUGH.

Day 66

"I can be changed by what happens to me but I refuse to be reduced by it."
~Maya Angelou

This Is My Time...

This is the appointed hour and time to take hold of my dreams and harness my will to make them happen. It is time to move beyond just surviving—this is my time to thrive. My health and happiness depend on my willingness and commitment to manifest the greatness that is me. I already possess everything I need to actualize every dream and goal I have ever conceived. The real factor is whether or not I am willing to take the road less traveled, or be content with following the path dictated by others. Myles Monroe reminds us in his book "Maximizing Your Potential" that, "We cannot become what we were born to be by remaining what we are."

It is my time to shine.
I AM ENOUGH.

Day 67

"Worthiness has no prerequisites. It's not an if/when proposition. True worthiness is as is."
~Brene Brown

Nothing to Prove...

Everyone's normal is different. To be different is not a negative. What is normal and natural for one person will be abnormal or odd to another. I accept all that makes me the unique individual that I am. I value and understand that my worth is not up for debate. My value was determined at birth. I have nothing to prove because I have already been affirmed at birth by God. The moment I forget this truth and attempt to prove my value, I lose my power. The only eyes of approval I need are the ones I see in the mirror.

I am an unrepeatable miracle.
I AM ENOUGH.

Day 68

"Never let life impede on your ability to manifest your dreams. Dig deeper into your dreams and deeper into yourself and believe that anything is possible, and make it happen."
~Corin Nemec

I Can Do It…

I am willing to be radical and bold with the vision I have been given. Goethe said of boldness that it has, "genius, power and magic in it." Life takes on new meaning when I live with the internal assurance that I am always divinely guided and protected. The fact that I am a person of power with the ability to create and recreate my life gives meaning to having belief. With this awareness, I can live the more abundant life of which Jesus. I no longer shrink from life when it presents new challenges, but I press boldly forward toward my vision in spite of the appearance of things. I rest in the assurance that divine protection is my birthright and that, regardless of how difficult things may appear, I can press on confidently, knowing that I have the power to make it.

I can accomplish great things with God as my guide.
I AM ENOUGH.

Day 69

"Do not come into agreement with fear. Activate your faith, live in victory, speak over your life and expect great things to come your way."
~Germany Kent

Living in Fullness...

My words are my bond to the Universe. The words I transmit into the Universe are a creative power. In essence, my words become law. What I confess with my tongue and believe in my heart is externalized in my life. I am a steward of my words. My power is connected to the words I speak, and these are the gateway to my destiny. It is through them that I set in motion the direction of my life. The Bible tells me that in the beginning there was the Word. First the thought, then the word, then the manifestation. I am the living word personified. Years ago, I would say that "sticks and stones may break my bones, but words will never harm me." This is absolutely not true. Words can heal or harm, build up or tear down. I have been either bolstered or hindered by words spoken to me or about me in my youth. These types of experiences often shape and affect how I live out my life experiences. Words are the vehicle through which life creates and evolves. What I think comes out in my communication.

My words have power.
I AM ENOUGH.

Day 70

"The only time you fail is when you fall down and stay down."
~Stephen Richards

Managing My Emotions...

The way I arrest fear is through refocusing my thoughts to those things I desire. I know that whatever I focus on will grow. If I focus on not fearing something, my focus remains on that which I do not desire, thereby, I keep the experience alive. Not living in fear requires daily attention. It requires spending regular time simply being still in order to connect to the wisdom within me. I can redirect my thoughts by writing down my hopes, reading inspirational material, listening to uplifting music, using positive affirmations, and being still. Everyone has the power to recharge his or her soul. As I shift my focus, I loosen the grip of fear. Refocusing my thoughts to a higher (positive) level shifts my mood. As my mood is shifted, my faith is activated. By keeping myself engaged in positive activities, I eliminate the entryway for fear. I should often dwell on the good things I desire—never giving prolonged attention to those things I don't want or that are negative. Napoleon Hill says that, "Positive and negative emotions cannot occupy the mind at the same time. One or the other must dominate. It is your responsibility to make sure that positive emotions constitute the dominating influence of your mind."

I focus on the positive.
I AM ENOUGH.

Day 71

"The most important thing to remember is this: To be ready at any moment to give up what you are for what you might become."
~W. E. B. DuBois

Rebirth...

I experience a rebirth as I remember who I am and why I am here. I was not created to suffer or to be an imitation of someone else. As Susan L. Taylor says, "You are a divine original." I was not created to live in lack. I was not created to live in fear. I was created to make manifest the gifts and talents that the Creator breathed into me to bless the earth.

I was created in love.
I AM ENOUGH.

Day 72

"The best way to not feel hopeless is to get up and do something. Don't wait for good things to happen to you. If you go out and make some good things happen, you will fill the world with hope, you will fill yourself with hope."
~Barack Obama

Renewed Hope...

Saint Augustine said, "For what is faith unless it is to believe what you do not see." My challenge is that, too often, I only believe what I see. Faith tells me that all things are possible if I believe. The belief element of faith is the foundation—my good will not come without belief. I build the latter by focusing thought and attention on those things I truly desire. It requires that I boldly proclaim to myself the things I am expecting. The only way to experience peace is to live a life of hopeful expectancy. Peace is a gift that only I can give to myself. No person or thing will give it to me. My bank account cannot give it to me, nor will my loved ones.

I work my faith.
I AM ENOUGH.

Day 73

"It is never too late to be what you might have been."
~George Eliot

Higher Power...

I have had many difficult moments in my life, but I have always made it through. Even when doubt and fear were overwhelming, I managed to keep going. When I wanted to give up, I kept going. When I could not see my way through, I kept going. As I wrestled with the negative chatter in my own head, I kept going. I kept going because deep down in my soul, I knew I was worth the effort. I realize now that everything I went through happened for a purpose. I am still here wounded and awaken, but I am now aware of my true value. My connection with a power Higher than me sustains and guides me always. I never have to fear because I know that with God, I am never alone.

I am a survivor.
I AM ENOUGH.

Day 74

"Inner peace begins the moment you choose not to allow another person or event to control your emotions."
~Pema Chodron

Releasing The Pain...

Anger and resentment are poisonous to the soul. The harm of harboring negative feelings is the negative ramifications on the host. It creates negative energy. Forgiveness is freedom to the host. It releases me from the bondage of the offense or pain. If I feel someone has wronged me, which placed me in a vulnerable position, I must practice the purest form of love, and that is forgiveness. For example, if I believe that my supervisor mistreated me, or my spouse cheated on me, or someone stole my money, the only way to free myself from the experience is through forgiveness. I must practice forgiveness so that I can move forward. I must first forgive myself for allowing the experience to happen and then I must forgive the offender.

Forgiveness allows me to move on.
I AM ENOUGH.

Day 75

"The cause of poverty is not scarcity. It is fear and small thinking."
~Alan Cohen

Creating Wealth...

I will develop a healthy relationship with money by paying what I owe. When I owe a debt, it is not only important that I pay it, but that I do so out of a place of gratitude. So, as I pay my monthly bills, I will remember to be thankful that I have the means to do so. I will relinquish the tendency to become annoyed and irritated when bills come in. I will acknowledge my debt and bless it, for it is not my enemy. I give things too much power when I run from them. Just as I created the debt, I have the ability and wherewithal to eliminate it, but I must first face it. I will write down all of my bills. I cannot fix what I will not face. Putting the light of day on my debt allows me to begin to take control. Also, I understand that, as I spend money, it will be replenished according to my faith. The reason some millionaires can lose their fortune and then gain it back is because they lost their money, not their wealth. To be wealthy is a mindset. A wealthy person knows that if they lose their money, they can always get it back again.

I am wealthy.
I AM ENOUGH.

Day 76

The greatest act of courage is to be and to own all of who you are — without apology, without excuses, without masks to cover the truth of who you are."
~Debbie Ford

I Am...

Life is really a process of remembering who and whose I am. Ralph Waldo Emerson said, "Oh Man! There is no planet, sun or star could hold you, if you but knew what you are." In the beginning, I was perfectly created. Who I was and what I was called to do on this earth was revealed to me when I was a little child. Life then happened, and over time I was given tainted feedback from my family and the culture about who I am supposed to be, which distracted me from my truth. As I began to receive these distorted messages, I attempted to conform to the expectations of others. Family members and teachers taught me who I am to be, while not paying attention to the person I was showing them. In my attempt to meet the expectations of others, I lost myself as I conformed to the ideals of those around me. This was when the struggle of life began. Deep inside I knew that who I appeared to be was not my true self. I became so accustomed to playing my role that I did not know how to be authentic. Vironika Tugaleva says, "You'll never know who you are unless you shed who you pretend to be."

I am who I am.
I AM ENOUGH.

Day 77

"You have power over your mind - not outside events. Realize this, and you will find strength."
~Marcus Aurelius

Gaining Strength...

Anytime I am experiencing difficulty in my life—whether it is my job, finances, relationship, or even health, I know that I am being prepared for a fuller life experience. Don't panic; breathe through it. Weightlifters know that when they are trying to take their body to another level, they increase the weight, and the key to lifting greater weight is proper breathing. When I am going through life growth cycles, and the weight of life gets heavier, I will focus on my breathing, not on the weight. If I do the latter, I will become overwhelmed. The key is to focus on my breath and push. I will get through whatever I am going through.

I breathe.
I AM ENOUGH.

Day 78

"Learn how to be happy with what you have while you pursue all that you want."
~Jim Rohn

Momentum...

When I shift my focus from what I can get to what I can give, I experience the abundance that Jesus spoke to us. Real abundance is serving humanity through my gifts and talents. As I share that which is a part of who I am, all good things return to me blessed and multiplied. I do not have to worry about how; I just know that when I give to life, life will always give to me exactly what I need.

I live in my abundance now.
I AM ENOUGH.

Day 79

"Thoughts have power; thoughts are energy. And you can make your world or break it by your own thinking."
~Susan L. Taylor

Unapologetically Me...

Life is always offering me the opportunity to expand into my truest self. Expansion requires that I stretch beyond where I currently am in order to discover all that I was meant to be.

My potential is limitless. I am a piece of God.
I AM ENOUGH.

Day 80

"There is no passion to be found playing small – in settling for a life that is less than the one you are capable of living."
~Nelson Mandela

Inner Peace...

Life is as I create it to be. This understanding places me in my rightful role as co-creator with the Universe. I know that I am not a victim of circumstance or doomed by conditions. Inner peace is my natural state. God did not form me to live in doubt, worry, or fear. I was formed from love and created for peace. What I have been calling my reality is actually a distorted illusion I have created with my mind. Armed with this new awareness, I can reprogram my mind to accept that even if I fall, God will catch me. With this assurance, I now know that I cannot fall too far where God cannot reach me. Knowing and believing this invites inner peace. As I acknowledge that God is on my side, nothing external can destroy the peace He offers.

I live in peace.
I AM ENOUGH.

Day 81

"God makes no mistakes. In all our trials and dramas there are lessons. Life is not a playground but a classroom. Our journey through life provides the coursework and the tests needed for our education and development."
~Susan L. Taylor

Blessings and Lessons…

So here I am at a turning point, seeking answers as I strive to understand and make sense of all the struggle and pain in my life. This voyage of self-discovery and understanding of my true self really unfolds as I begin the process of peeling back all the layers of falsehoods and inaccurate information I have been taught. The philosopher Nietzsche said, "He who has a why to live for can bear almost any how." Knowing that there is a reason for every adversity I experience gives me the fortitude to persevere. I understand that my life experiences do not just happen to me but through me, based on my beliefs. I'm always mindful that I live in a spiritual Universe. This is God's world subject to universal laws and principles He has established, and many of the painful experiences I deem as tragedies in my life are, in reality, transitions.

Life is always in divine order.
I AM ENOUGH.

Day 82

"To be yourself in a world that is constantly trying to make you something else is the greatest accomplishment."
~Ralph Waldo Emerson

Centered in Truth...

The most important gift I can give myself is to be who I am. As I center myself in this truth, I discover the strength, courage, and wisdom to fulfill my life's purpose. In this state, I can hear and receive guidance from my heart. I am encouraged by and equipped with the wisdom to create the experiences that are in alignment with my greater good. In this place of truth, I step into the flow of existence where life is no longer a struggle but a consistent movement forward.

My life is God's gift to me.
I AM ENOUGH.

Day 83

"One of the greatest tragedies in life is to lose your own sense of self and accept the version of you that is expected by everyone else."
~K.L. Toth

Removing The Mask...

As a human, I desire to be secure, to know that I am going to be okay and that I will have enough food, shelter, love, etc. I search for security in things like jobs, money, homes, cars, and relationships. I also seek security in my religion, customs, and traditions. When these things that have become so ingrained in me are threatened, there is fear in not knowing what tomorrow will bring. I am taught to fear lack, to fear differences, to fear dying, to fear being alone—the list is endless. The deeper message conveyed here is that I am not enough. And because I often do not feel I am enough, that somehow I am inadequate, I begin to wear a mask of deception to attempt to cover up who I actually think I am. As such, I present myself to the world by playing a role and wearing a mask that I believe is acceptable. In the process, I lose myself. I very often grow attached to the mask and fear that I won't be loved and accepted if I am not what others believe I should be. It is only when I am alone, and the mask is off that I feel the effects of not living authentically. I find myself feeling empty, depressed, and unfulfilled as my soul hungers to be nurtured and released. It is time to take off the mask so that I can release the shame, doubt, insecurity, anger, pain, and low self-esteem that has been hindering me from being my best.

Everyone is my equal.
I AM ENOUGH.

Day 84

"Never be afraid to trust an unknown future to a known God."
~Corrie ten Boom

Faith It...

Faith is believing that life is on our side even when what is happening to us doesn't make sense. To "believe" is a verb, and a verb denotes action. To say that I believe and then not act is synonymous with mental assent. Believing is receiving in Spirit before it is manifested in the physical. Nothing is accomplished without belief. Hope anticipates something that cannot be had until God brings it to pass. The law of life is belief. How I think dictates my experience. The light of faith allows me to move through this life experience unencumbered. I understand that all things are working for my good. True surrender requires faith and courage to release my habitual patterns of behavior and thought. It is only through letting go of the old that I can open up to the new. It is only when I surrender to all I discover that I experience the peace which surpasses all understanding. As I surrender, I know that all is well. Surrendering allows the soul to come into greater alignment with God. When I quiet my mind, I tap into a power that is not limited by my five senses. This internal power allows me to see the invisible. Faith is evidenced in every human being. For most, that faith light is dim; however, I need only turn it up to experience the very substance for which I hope. Faith releases what was already present. It allows God's energy to move in my life.

I walk in faith.
I AM ENOUGH.

Day 85

"When we attach value to things that aren't love—the money, the car, the house, the prestige—we are loving things that can't love us back. We are searching for meaning in the meaningless."
~Marianne Williamson

Managing My Environment...

I am the CEO of my life, and there are times when I have to fire and demote those that are hindering my progression. In order to become the best version of myself, I must manage those who I allow access to my life. I understand that relationships can either propel me forward or stifle my growth. There are only 24 hours in a day, and I cannot afford to spend time engaging with those that deplete my energy or distract me with things that are not fruitful. The fact is, not everyone in my circle is good for my environment. Negative and complacent people create atmospheres that are toxic to my well-being. They tend to sprinkle seeds of doubt, fear, and even envy. Sometimes they are long term friends and even family members. As I commit to loving myself completely, I must decide to fire some people from life and love others from afar.

I allow only positive energy in my life.
I AM ENOUGH.

Day 86

"Let nothing dim the light that shines from within."
~Maya Angelou

I Affirm...

I am here now to be and experience peace and wholeness. There is no other time but now that matters. I decide where my life leads and how I choose to show up. I see each moment as a fresh start. I am no longer confined to who I thought I was. Today I declare, unapologetically, that I am enough!

My life is a blessing.
I AM ENOUGH.

Day 87

"Everybody can be great...because anybody can serve. You don't have to have a college degree to serve. You don't have to make your subject and verb agree to serve. You only need a heart full of grace. A soul generated by love."
~Martin Luther King Jr.

Being of Service...

When I shift my focus from what I can get to what I can give, I experience the abundance that Jesus spoke to us. Real abundance is serving humanity through my gifts and talents. As I share, all good things return to me blessed and multiplied. I do not have to worry about how; I just know that when I give to life, life will always give to me exactly what I need.

As I give I receive.
I AM ENOUGH.

Day 88

"Why are you trying so hard to fit in when you were born to stand out?"
~Ian Wallace

No Struggle...

Real life fulfillment is rooted in simplicity. Filling my life with things only makes my existence more complex. I appreciate the gift of living well—nice homes, automobiles, etc.—but sometimes I over-extend myself to have more. I clutter my life with things which occupy so much of my energy that peace escapes me. My life becomes overwhelming as I focus on figuring out how not to lose the things I have. These things then become a source of pain and irritation. I focus too much on getting possessions that I then struggle to pay for and maintain. As I grow in awareness of truth, things no longer have the power I once given to them. I know that bigger square footage or a foreign vehicle can never bring me lasting joy. I am reminded that I always have a choice, and can live from a place of either love or fear. When I "listen softly," as a dear friend once reminded me, I am guided to the truth. There is no struggle in truth. Many of us have been taught and told that life has to be a struggle. It does not. It becomes a struggle when I'm not living from my center—my heart.

Listening softly connects me to my source.
I AM ENOUGH.

Day 89

"The first step towards getting somewhere is to decide you're not going to stay where you are."
~John Pierpont "J.P." Morgan

Limitless...

A fresh start—a new beginning is what each breath of life offers me. I am given the gift to shed old thoughts, beliefs, and patterns that kept me bound in the past. In this moment, fueled with new information and clear revelation, I can start again with a clean slate. Not limited by my past, I can live a life that is in harmony with my truth. What is true is that every moment offers me an opportunity to begin anew. Every breath offers me a new beginning to start again. I am no longer tied to the pain that has kept me repeating the same lessons over and over again, but I now move in the newness that is always available right here, right now. It is my rebirthing. The good news is that I do not have to wait for an appointed time or event to live better. I can experience new life immediately.

I am starting afresh.
I AM ENOUGH.

Day 90

"Life is a matter of choices, and every choice you make makes you."
~John C. Maxwell

The Choice is Mine...

I have found that, in my pursuit for a richer life, I often find myself discouraged and frustrated as it seems the more I push for greater achievement, the more the increasingly abundant life of which Jesus spoke eludes me. The reality is that, when I have allowed myself to accept certain conditions over an extended time, I forget that I always have a choice, no matter how desperate or challenging the situation might appear. Poverty or power is a choice! The good news is that I no longer have to live with lack and limitation. The wise elders say, "If you knew better, you would do better."

Today, I know better.
I AM ENOUGH.

www.ingramcontent.com/pod-product-compliance
Lightning Source LLC
LaVergne TN
LVHW051557070426
835507LV00021B/2619